Hallelujah Blackout

Also by Alex Lemon

Mosquito

Hallelujah Blackout

Alex Lemon

MILKWEED EDITIONS

Published 2008 by Milkweed Editions
Printed in Canada
Cover design by Brad Norr Design
Cover painting, "[you who were never there]" by Natalie Salminen Rude
Author photo by Ariane Balizet
Interior design by Wendy Holdman, Prism Publishing Center
The text of this book is set in Rotis Serif.
08 09 10 11 12 5 4 3 2 1
First Edition

Milkweed Editions, a nonprofit publisher, gratefully acknowledges sustaining support from Anonymous; Emilie and Henry Buchwald; the Bush Foundation; the Patrick and Aimee Butler Family Foundation; CarVal Investors; the Dougherty Family Foundation; the Ecolab Foundation; the General Mills Foundation; the Claire Giannini Fund; John and Joanne Gordon; William and Jeanne Grandy; the Jerome Foundation; Dorothy Kaplan Light and Ernest Light; Constance B. Kunin; Marshall BankFirst Corp.; Sanders and Tasha Marvin; the May Department Stores Company Foundation; the McKnight Foundation; a grant from the Minnesota State Arts Board, through an appropriation by the Minnesota State Legislature, a grant from the National Endowment for the Arts, and private funders; an award from the National Endowment for the Arts, which believes that a great nation deserves great art; the Navarre Corporation; Debbie Reynolds; the Starbucks Foundation; the St. Paul Travelers Foundation; Ellen and Sheldon Sturgis; the Target Foundation; the Gertrude Sexton Thompson Charitable Trust (George R. A. Johnson, Trustee); the James R. Thorpe Foundation; the Toro Foundation; Moira and John Turner; United Parcel Service; Joanne and Phil Von Blon; Kathleen and Bill Wanner; Serene and Christopher Warren; the W. M. Foundation; and the Xcel Energy Foundation.

Special funding for this book was provided by the Jerome Foundation.

Library of Congress Cataloging-in-Publication Data

Lemon, Alex.
  Hallelujah blackout / Alex Lemon.
  — 1st ed.
    p.   cm.
ISBN 978-1-57131-431-4 (pbk. : acid-free paper)
  I. Title.
  PS3612.E468H35 2008
  811'.6—dc22

                          2007046469

This book is printed on acid-free paper.

MINNESOTA
STATE ARTS BOARD

NATIONAL
ENDOWMENT
FOR THE ARTS

jerome
foundation

For my families

Contents

Acknowledgments

Thank you to all of my wonderful friends and family for their continued love and support—Ma and Bob, Dad and Lindy, Nick Flynn, Mark Conway, and Jeff Shotts (for the bucketloads of doom, poetry help, love, and gnomes), Ray Gonzalez, Simone Perrin, Amanda Nadelberg, Beth Bachmann, Rick Barot, Mark Doty and Paul Lisicky, Julie Schumacher, Kathleen Glasgow, Paul Otremba, Amy Williams, Michael and Claire, the Harmes family, Craig Morgan Teicher, Brenda Shaughnessy and Cal, Casey Golden, Polly Carden, Jess Grover, Nancy Palmeri, Adam Clay, Tim O'Keefe, Matt Hart, Matt Henriksen, Erin Sindberg-Porter, Lars Bierly, David Hernandez, Lisa Glatt, Tony Lacavaro, Aaron Baker, Keith Ekiss, Jake Keeler, Chris Koza, Laurel Havas, Keenan Sue, Jason Shannon, Kevin Duggan, Rich Albrecht, Paul Gillis; my Macalester Scot teammates, students, colleagues, and peers; Meg Storey, Lee Montgomery, Rob Spillman, Emily Bliquez, and finally, the MFA program in creative writing at the University of Minnesota.

I'm also grateful to everyone at Milkweed Editions—this book wouldn't be possible without their remarkable work and kindness, and Jim Cihlar's unwavering editorial diligence, insight, and humor.

And I am forever indebted to Ariane Balizet, for everything she does—amazing me endlessly—for putting up with me each and every day.

Many thanks to the editors of the following publications where these poems first appeared, sometimes in earlier versions:

Another Chicago Magazine: "Orgazo MoMo"

Arson: "The Meat Grinder"

Artful Dodge: "In This Best of All Possible Worlds" and "When You Don't Know . . ."

Barn Owl Review: "Yet I Ride the Little Horse"

Black Warrior Review: "Abracadaver," "And No More May I Be," "Boomerang," "Boxboard," "Chronocentrism," "Drilling Tiny Holes in My Head," "Homebound," "It's Always Late Where You Are," "Rally Rally Rally," and "Roundworm"

BOMB: "Skin On Skin Off Skin On Skin Off"

The Brooklyn Rail: "Interview with a Ghost" and "Sing"

Cannibal: "Fuck All This Merrymaking"

Coconut: "Flourishing"

Copper Nickel: "The Lights Go On The Lights Go Off"

Dragonfire: "I Love Cake," "My Pet Chicken," "Plication," and "So Soon"

Five Fingers Review: "underlife"

Flights: "The Night Diego Maradona Tried"

Florida Review: "Praxis," "Rocksteady," and "The Way It Is"

Forklift, OH: "Asthma Attack," "Elevator Music," "Good Times," and "Resurrection"

Gulf Coast: "Sawing Tinfoil"

Hotel Amerika: "Etiology"

Indigest: "It's Hard To Tell Who Will Love You the Best" and "Spotless"

The Journal: "Better Cleaning with Voodoo"

The Kenyon Review: "Patter to Mend"

Knock: "Modern Man's Hustle"

Mantis: "Up All Night"
Open City: "Dourine"
Pebble Lake Review: "All We Inherit," "Up," and "Wildfires"
Prairie Schooner: "Chévere"
Redactions: "Operculum"
Saltgrass: "Sizzler"
Smartish Pace: "Bedbugs," "Everything," and "Something Wicked This Way Comes"
Washington Square: "Souvenirs from the Unraveling"

Excerpts of "Hallelujah Blackout" have appeared in *AGNI, BOMB, Black Warrior Review, Coconut, The Concher, Copper Nickel, Denver Quarterly, Dislocate, Forklift, OH, Gulf Coast, Interim, Marginalia, New Orleans Review, Open City, Pebble Lake Review, Saltgrass, Tin House*, and *Typo*, many times in radically different shapes than what appears here, and occasionally in versions that have simply disappeared.

Excerpts of "Abracadaver" were performed with the artist Jake Keeler at the Walker Art Center in Minneapolis, Minnesota in an event funded by MNartists.org.

"Abracadaver" appeared in a different form as a chapbook in *Black Warrior Review*.

Hallelujah Blackout

underlife

after H. L. Hix

nothing is harder than hiding
in the dark buckets & mason jars

heavy
      & split with nails
the lightbulb swerving   small

            charities
& shaken, the bramble-running
deer   vein   & streak

this place so full of people
fucked
        up & hollow

the sound in the cellar: writhing
     faces upturned

to the plum-glut sky   be shackled
     to the selves you squander

    the dirt sings
no less   than those you save

A Pit—but Heaven over it—
And Heaven beside, and Heaven abroad,
and yet a Pit—
With Heaven over it.

Emily Dickinson

Sing

Shadows dizzy the rabbits
& this is welcome
To the great state
Of nowhere—WE MAKE
MEEK ADJUSTMENTS
That blank before bang—
The pills kicking in. I will
Demonstrate with puppets
I will repeat myself
Again & again
In a bedroom
Always swirling & lit
It is the existence
Of circus bears unicycling
In the belly
A lifetime of melting
Inside my chest & a voice
Kick drumming
Through my sleep
A blurry windowsill lined
With things that will die
So, again: we can
Wish but we'll still
Drown in the river
Are you listening?
In the pearl-
Branched river
& that right there
Is the glass

That will tip
From the table
When we move
A percussive
Slap that covers
The mouth—the good
Silence before the you-
Are-not-going-home

Flourishing

Car doors, bricks, a drill press—
I've broken my hands thousands of times

because I'm afraid of what they can do.
Seizures of black-and-white photos,

sixteen-millimeter film. Flash,
flash and framed in spider-leg light.

Smile falsely and the piano hammers
unbearably loud. Is it a stream of blood

or a forgotten plant's winged roots?
When I die brokenhearted, bandages

will muffle the paradise I choke
from your electric fence, but know

that I knocked, openmouthed in a sarabanding
rain. Your Christmas cactus will bloom

fluorescent—terrible beauties will appear
on the orphaned child's tongue.

Rocksteady

It's so burly in the sky but there's no time
To speak about the sparkling lovelies
With all the broken windows and you reaching
For a shard to bleedout your arm. If only the walls
Could tell you the angle for the perfect falling
Of sunlight, but hey man, shit happens—soon
We'll all have grown wings and be away from this
Place rolling with hospital beds. Blinds like ribs,
And if you didn't know better, yeah, we all look
Like someone you used to know. Nobody
Answers the door and the bathroom lights wink
On and off. On and off. So if it's you
Rummaging within this theater, would that
Make you a me, breathing inside a we?
That symphony. That freak show.
This cathedral of zodiacs and sad songs,
I love it. We will miss this neighborhood
Big-loving with the down-and-out and car-part
Castles. Ooh, now can you see the good time
My way? I'm not asking you what you know
About yourself, but what's on
The face of the one who follows you
Around handing out pieces of darkness
As you plead with the trees. Turn to the last
Page in the brochure of sleep as you go in
With the rest of the beautiful corpses.
Take your seats and blow kisses please.
Stare—the obvious isn't so topless.

Sing *mercy mercy kiss the pigs, tongues all out*
For the strangler figs, then open your chest to let
Me in. And no fiddling with the endoscope—
There must be silence during the performance.

So Soon

You will wheel around the corner
into the bathroom and come

face to face with your nude self cradling
a severed Barbie head and a bucket spilling

over with slivered mango. The neighbor's blue-lit
porch will shiver when you speak to yourself

dreams of the deep flash of barracuda—
the best way to haul thousands of pounds

of fabricating equipment—bolts and nails,
endless highways of steel ribbon.

Shadows will swing, armed with great hammers,
and you'll shave each other's heads

again and again. Tornados of wrens
will crack yield signs in adoration of the horizon—

its towing up of the sun. You'll both grow
like glass and smaller, more

and more sleepy. Please don't think
I'm in love with the way you swear.

For a long time I have wanted nothing
more than to bring this to your attention.

Operculum

Today I wore my best flesh suit streetwalking—
velvet back, forty-footers and tulips dying
in the city's cross-piped machinery.
Cats barked from brownstone windows
and on a boom box the mayor
demanded more baby making. I itched
my birthright, banned beef from my belly.
But to really feel the smog you had to roll
around in it. The leaves—the difficulty of sunlight.
Imagine the sidewalks' spiky oysters, hydrants
caked with old. But when the vendors held up
their bottles of piss I yelped because I knew
it had to be time for the examination.
At the hospital, a nurse helped me
cope with the probing. And it was true
what the pamphlet said about my
troubles—first-degree burns,
blisters bubbled on my calves. But these days
I have little time to let mere ailments worry me.
My past is ass-kicking its way
into my sleep. I know—right now,
everyone behind me is everywhere
they might possibly be, and all
at the same time. And again,
right outside the subway I grow
light-headed and have to grab the railing—
there is a heaving in dusk's wobbly trees,
everyone slurping on ice pops, clearing
their throats—a cacophony that leads

me to believe there is a reason for all
the switched babies. Without a slipped
chainsaw or our fingertips on the wild-
bottomed clouds as our heart convulses
one last time, the next blink might make us
midnight with the smile & machete—
we, tangoing into the endless.

Praxis

Let us blink at the windows
That never fully close—that make
Us doubletake at row upon row of piled-

Up dead things. The flicker
Of today's favors will keep us
From washing our bodies

For weeks, impregnate us
With a certain occasion of light.
In the humid rain we'll grow

With color but that is not
What I want to be destroyed
By. I will have to sleep

With the radio on, listen
To the laughter of passing
Clouds. I hope someday to learn

A new sort of silence—the beauty
In absence or what will never
Be. But at least today, all the front

Yards piled with leaves
In this city are homes
Waiting for burning.

And No More May I Be

So this is calamity: calendula-
oiled hands cupping a mouth

that sings through the caving-
away thunderlight as the weeks

keep swinging by—house finches
shivering groundward in the catgut

blight. Black boughs absent of any
living weights. In the rain a man

ducks into his coat to light a smoke.
The park bitter with echoing space.

The park freezing. In the rain a man
ducks into his coat like the split-

ribbed chest of a dead horse
swallowing a wet-cheeked boy.

Benches slick red. Benches freezing.
In the rain a soaked man

watching in the rain. In the rain
my hands pink hands numb

in the rain. Beneath the skin
a humming *is*. Geese wreathed

in their own winter-coming
breath. Skinhulled. Taut

skin bustling. Bottle caps old
buttons half-buried hard in the dirt.

Requiem

The pie-throated voices of smashed men
        spiral out endlessly from animals glaring

from the roadside: hollow-bodied dogs. Those
        whisky-colored collies that sprint to the end of
gravel driveways, tongues grape splotched,

        slack—their *Think of this & tremble* barks. Head
gaping with barks. Two calico cats in a picture

        window watch very still in morning's sunshine.
Crinkleroot hung with boltrope from the eaves.
        Red-winged blackbirds high on slumped

power lines. *Who will watch of the holes in the sky,*
        they harp, lifting from one claw to the other.

Dark air unfurled dark air lowing apart your easy
        shapes, they sing through dawn through
the ever-broken light of morning going

        on. Another lands in front of my moving
car. *Jubilee,* it goes, in a burst of fluttering

        color, under & back from my swerving
away. Another peeks lofty from a blue-walled
        playhouse, slow dancing its perch—*lustral*

Sleepwalkers slip away lockdown. The lawns
    squeaky green, children holding hands
as they look up & smile, waiting for the bus.

Modern Man's Hustle

after Jake Keeler

Raw with nightsweats in the morning, & rocked
& ravaged by the spring downpour,
We winnowed our way to a place
Neon signed, a road narrowly
Curved with sweetbriar & passing cars
Whose drivers saluted us, waved a thumbs up.
While we slept, someone had shaved
Our eyebrows off & written on us
With a Sharpie. The makeup we bought
At Kum & Go was made from berries. This,
The God in the dashboard rumbled, brings you
Closer to Mother Earth. Bullshit, I sang,
Because I wanted more malt-liquor
Time. I wanted Pac-Man and Hot Tamales.
The cousin of a car fire, the blisters
That form on fingertips from ringing
Someone's doorbell until the police show up
To play your ribs like a xylophone.
It must have been entertaining
To see our mouths drop when they sentenced us.
If only they'd seen us earlier—standing on the porch
Tugging our balls. Surely, that would have brought
The house down. But in this life, we must
Be sure never to ask for too much info
About who we really are. You know
What I mean, brother? For too many years
We will be driven to this country-road ditch
To pick up cigarette butts & Bud Light cans

With the rest of the orange-clad dummies.
It's in our eyes now—that whatever
Is meant to be is shit to me—hands scoured
Over & over until there can't be fingerprints
Or warmth. The drips. Of blessings,
Unwrapped & tossed. Faces sunsetting,
Blurred windows. The streaks. The blessings.

When You Don't Know
If It's Really the Good Stuff

Our eyes were cherry red and we scratched, rested
And scratched, before realizing we'd taken too many
Muscle relaxers. To test our hypothesis we made

Very sinuous love. Our lawn chairs were bodies
Our bodies shouted about dolphins. We tagged each other
With darts and followed each other like private dancers

By the time we reached home the tranquilizers
Had kicked in and someone was always helping
Themselves to apples and beans. Each day

We followed the mailman as he walked
From hospital to hospital, feeling the blood
Vessels tear in our thighs. But the good news

Never came and now we are broke
And our schematics are useless
We walk the mall carrying fifty-pound bags

Of heart attacks. Triple cheeseburgers and triple
Bypass. We must keep moving, the handsome woman
Behind us going swish-swish with the metal detector

Chronocentrism

If we were somewhere
better doubts would still

loiter & spill even
when a good thing
happens you are

the sun   coming up
copper-plated irises—
shovel-buried we start again

each morning with nothing
but corduroy shoulders

to laugh on mouths
to kiss open when
better we are lounging

in dirty dirty shadows the
birds of paradise look good

enough not to move
so when you feel your
legs again you can go

haunt all the couch
sleepers with hypnosis

blundering when they walk
away where crying ruby eyed
they'll better shoot & be

Boxboard

Inside this fullness   I am
    the kind of guy .   who makes

engine purrs & slaps   the water
    surface   imagining oars

shorn from Norway maples
    the hours—   so close   behind

me   merge   trills & whistles
    through open   windows

shorter-closed   to a room   where
    I bathe   this melody

& bedlam   spilling   on & on
    the clamor   of sirens

outside   & comfort   in
    what you can't see   of yourself

when some sort   of healing
    is longed for   echoing

again & again   & as best it can
    the slouching   body

    listens   back

Roundworm

for Tony

When the monsters start dropping
      Visine in their eyes & stumble
down the brownstone steps into Saturday

night's severe lamppost glare, please stay
      home with the freshly picked Granny
Smith apples—make a dozen pies, spin

so much lettuce dry your hands prune.
      With the radio turned up
it's hard to keep track of anything—

neon zigging from the sky, burying
      in the water-shaking elms—
leaves helicoptering to the curbs. Outside

it's the kingdom of wandering around
      in the dark & roughhousing—
my forehead gashed against the glass.

Feathered hedges still damp
      with the afternoon showers.
The same bat circles the pretty house

mistaking the same black-painted attic
      window for something dry. I think
I need to follow you around, it says

swooping down & again at passersby.
   On the other side of the glass you throw
darts, your shirt incredibly bluewhite

beneath the flashing. Above the streetlights hissing
      awake down the block, a cello-soft
glow opens like veins through the spruce.

Homebound

Tonight, in the flustery
scowls of the neighbor-
hood, house parties
thump snuffed
out, kids fight
in the street
with rods they yanked
from grandma's curtains
& something in
the backyard
of my mind
is as murky as
summer noons
that reek
of the humming
roughneck's breath.
Hands clap & shadows
from the trees scatter.
Bad guitar & *timber—*
the blood sugar
drops without hard
candy. When cars pull
up or away. When car
doors slam—bodies
curl into themselves
& smaller & like a biting
worm, that mind-moored
thing comes full circle in
the stilling dark

& starts eating its own
tail. First taste
& everything swells—
shards of the yellow
moon, the radiator
forever banging.

The Night Diego Maradona Tried

for Bernard Balizet

to die & didn't, or not yet, or won't, no matter
how much Pele pleads. & after the news rolled
back into the radio, voices burst
outside my window & something busted
into my room. Puffing delirious, I cowered
in bed, desert faced & sleepless. Somewhere,
Diego was dying. Heart so filled with cocaine
silt & dreams of sex-romping on soccer balls,
only the short skirt or testicle-tight pant
of a nurse might force him to breathe.
I won't lie. My walls smell like meat.
Deli sandwiches. I won't lie, I have no legs
& sit in bed counting my firmness for days.
Goal! Goal! Goal! I scream as I pound
hoofprints into the ceiling. I call them game plans.
I call them lovely. I call them home
for bagpipe lovin'. This, I blame on peaceful thoughts,
the source of all ruined, fizzless colas.
Corner kick or fucking people over—
that's what we all are, angry hearts
banging away like steroid-filled moths
at a zap bulb. Addicted, verging on mourning,
we hope this is not what it feels like to die,
as outside, sirens roar up dreams of Albuquerque
& five bullet-riddled minutes on *Cops*, that chalky
taste cartwheeling on the tongue—oh, how the last bite
of a Big Mac makes you want to slit throats.

Yet 1 Ride the Little Horse

After I put my arm around the dead
swordfish that hung like a colossal slick bell

I felt blood blossoming in my cheeks when
from the cracked & serrated mouth I thought

I heard a voice tell me the world was well
past over. I wanted nothing more during the flash

of that picture being taken than complete
deafness. Drenched & fully clothed, a woman

on the dock shook her head from side to side.
A broken minnow bucket turned upside down shone

like a rain-softened pumpkin until we drank
so much we could no longer speak & kicked it

in the lagoon. But now, lying on the couch, so tired
after dancing around the room by myself, staring

at the half-open Hawaiian shirt, the shock in his warbling
eyes in the picture, I remember: the dead thing really

whispered something terrifically soft—a strain that bent
out & up through the palm trees when I pushed

my fingers through its gills & a horrific light burst
all around, blinking me, & in the white sun I was ashen,

counting the wondrous things that bobbed along—
split two headed & barely listening as I went down.

Boomerang

My waking mouth glues
shut in the middle
of the night & from the crocus
break lifting shapes, purple
darkening a darker air.
I don't recognize
the comfortable
superstitions my hands
wolf when I wave them
in front of my face.
There is no way these
are mine, I think—no
fucking way.
Holding them up
to the blue buzzing
light that kills all
of the whirling bugs
on the porch, their out-
lines pulse—
& rummaging through
the toolshed, I think,
whoever's they might
be, they sure as shit
can't stay here.

It's Always Late Where You Are

for M. S.

O timorous warnings—underlife of lures & late

      shuffling lurkers—colossal gullet
        of pink-bottomed clouds

      I do not   no matter   how whole

      tomorrow's maybe magic: swollen

lymph glands & chewed-away hands—a darker
      than midnight thing above

the city's ovation of deep-
      breathing sleepers   see

      that it cannot be done—

      to describe this pale-
         ness—

agnail & ankles   dressed
      in the wet sumac I'm here—

      going to be vaulting out

Abracadaver

I'm locked in my bedroom so send back the clowns.
My clone wears a brown shirt, and I seduce him when
there's no one around.
Mano a mano on a bed of nails.

TV on the Radio

I

thank you again
      for the broken

& inevitable engineering—
      the all-important

choking on love
        how I love

splitting open—my good
      god damn *now*—

      the violent effects
        of coming

speckled with rust
      & flakes & crumbling

II

lotus-hipped flesh eater
    crimson tongued

I fail shellrotted
    through this burling

cascades of delicate bodies—
    let me celebrate that

boundless beauty
    with hot needles

mouthfuls of tarantula
    pudding

III

what I give will determine
    what blessing

I might receive so it's two
    for one at the midway

& I will go on forever doing
    incomprehensible things—

the horseflies ladder up
    the ferris wheel

O cardinal-lit moon   we're all going
    to be right there—
        that whispering dirt—

I love how you taste
    each time

I feel a draft & do nothing
    but loll my dead-end tongue

IV

in a knifing away
        of the skin
your kisses appear—

that delicate meat
      without bone—

a finger-splitting taste
      between torn & filled

terribly   little
     boys   little boys

the midnight
     sparrows
         whimper

V

please someone please
    tell me how
        much flesh can

be tolerated
    day after day—

I will put
        anything
in my mouth

VI

darker   I say darker—
    burstswept

every fucking   where

the silver-spotted sun
         in my sleeves—

so grind baby grind
    because momma needs

honey   a few more
       swerving turns

lockjawed   & laid
    down turning further

       & further away

VII

neither bleached nor
    beautiful in the cellar

my blueberry-bushed insides
    are graveled with wants—

a mobile twisted from coat
    hangers over a darkness

swings   of course this means
    we are dying all a bit closer

VIII

spiral fractures & fireworks
    even in this world

baby girls flirt
    with their daddies

medicine chests filled blue
    with cuts & bruises

I'll take your overcoat shaved
    head my sober accordion

happy to tell me even the trees
    are ashamed to watch

& the cold cold
    ground is rawboned on fire

IX

a coterie of fishhooks
  spine my hands
   to the dictionary

billygoats groan with pleasure
struggling in the barbed wire

  & everything–everything
   around us burns

X

listen here
    my A-felonied friends—

when before
    you go   the skins

porch swinging   I believe

    in apparitions
       myself halved

all around me   black world—

    there is a trying—
       ashpowder for easy
         fingertasting

love houses stormed
    with pitchforks   relentless
       this pounding

from inside my chest
    a pit-graved *here*

XI

we sit at tables shuddering
  about the nethery pageant
    of bones

beneath our feet—
  their thousand ways to hold
    hands in the dark

& so we hang fillets of each
  caught horse in the front yard—
    armatures of barbed wire—

their eight-ball eyes when they
  go barely remembering
    how it used to be

XII

O riffraff
    of block-wandering

needs   lushed pink
    & always

ready to burst   O pretty
    beasts   we pray

for good luck
    & riddance

mouths floppy in passing
    cars   filled more

with gasoline than fire
    all of us   where

the fuck have you
    been   suffering

nothing & suffering
    the fish bellies

turned purple white
    & red inside out

XIII

for these days are kissless
    lips & wire

something making love

    to us
        while we twitch

in our sleep   wanting
    in our silence

      a reverie

silk-knotted wrists
    kindly split throats

XIV

the day cherry lipped
    & aching away

        with ground-up light

the riverbed washes
    with a thousand doll heads
      their XX eyes

singing such a fine time to be
      broken & swayed

O caved-in heads   held
      to your ear

      O heavy breathing

XV

& I cannot stop
   asking   for gifts

that only buckle me
   which had seemed

in this brilliant waste
      of snow

lovely & hopeless
   loved & irrevocably lost

XVI

at night when the deer feed
    from my insides

but only you
        drink
    milk & blood

from my half-animaled
            breasts

    for hours I'll work my breath
        into sirens—

how many times
    will I have to streak
myself   down
        your cheeks

Upon the steep floor flung from dawn to dawn
The silken skilled transmemberment of song;

Permit me voyage, love, into your hands . . .

Hart Crane

Up All Night

Mayflies zapped good-bye
above the window ledge
where vacant-eyed pigeons
clucked *huh uh huh*
about dusk swamping
over the city & for a split
second, my face mashed
against the screen door,
I understood everything—
dumb things that run electric
toward a man who will put them
down, the never-sleeping
body. To see if I really could go
on I tugged at each tooth
to make sure they'd still tear
meat, stood in the dry & darkened
shower waving a lighter
in front of the shaving mirror.
But so tired I was with the tiny
muscles, all out of clean
sweatshop T-shirts, that soon
I needed every socket plugged
in & on. The monster truck rally,
all the radios crackling.
What's up what's up I answered the heavy-
breathing phone &, after lying about my age
& imagining a birthday party angelic
with willowy light, told the voice
to leave me alone. *You should see*

my face, I said. *I have nothing else to say.*
There must be better places to be,
I thought, sticking a chopstick down
the cast to scratch the fire that had erupted
in that smelly murk. One of these times
I'm going to surely fall, I grimaced, crashing
obliviously into the workbench as I spun
around & around. But nothing would stop
the tingling. The music man in my head
was saying it again & louder. Go,
he shouted. Go goddamn it, go!

All We Inherit

for Matt

what I found in the whites
of my eyes was everything
that's come before. disco.
aluminum baseball bats
spidering the windshield
of a Volvo. the story
my parents never told—
in truth, anybody could have
been that guy. the bad guy.
the butterface. with that
in my head only seventeen
days were found in the new
month I made by walking
backwards around the block
whispering your name
into my mittens. smoke
from the gutters. smoke
from my mouth. the collar
of my shirt: fur. dandruff
speckled. I don't care
how ugly she is, her chest
pocked with burnout stars.
I'll kiss her anyway, I thought
humming as I skipped
through the sliding doors—
because the rabbit light
is all around us, right?
whoa boy—let me

tell you a little about
what man troubles himself
with, the security guard
at the bank said, cowing
his arm around my neck
as he took what little I had
in my hands and turned
me back around.

Souvenirs from the Unraveling

for D. H.

The owner's manual mother gave me
Taught me everything I needed to know
Up to this point, so I didn't realize
It was too late until they phoned
About organ donation. Then came the dull
Ache of heartburn. Then the parade of mice.
I tried to rid myself of the infestation
By walking miles with a sandwich board.
I wished everyone a terrific stay.
Cars passed, horns honked wildly.
Many folks gave me the finger.
One woman pulled down her top,
But I am a waver, and I smiled, gave
Her the thumbs up. I sat next to a brick wall
Painted with wet graffiti. *Kiss,* it said
In big orange letters. I thought, this is cool,
But the letters were so fat and squished together,
It might have said *kill.* This was very sad,
So I stared into the sun to erase the memory.
This is what they do in movies and really good books.
Actually, the stride was the sort of flapping
Dance heated ribosomes do under microscopes.
I remembered this from Sunday school
Or an infomercial about knives.
Needless to say, the day was furious
With flashbacks. The concrete grew condensation,
I stepped in never-ending piles of gum.
My favorites were purple and tasted like grape

Or the van Gogh I licked repeatedly as a child.
Nightfall and I was at the shore with a number
Of half-scratched lotto tickets and a very old
Burrito. This is my sort of magic, I reflected,
Squawking melodies from my kazoo.
But it was time to say hello again to the many things
I had said good-bye to. I blew a tornado
Of kisses to friends—sand crabs,
The gutter worms. I wished the others—
All the floating diapers and Depends,
The sweetest of dreams. I spoke my prayers
To the yummy and listened to the pounding waves
Jibber-jabber that even after today,
There was all of endless tomorrow to go.

Rally Rally Rally

When I tried to say goodnight they came carving
with Bowie knives. When I tried to brawl they cut
off my eyelids, they took my sight. So the nightlife
goes sometimes. & sometimes, no matter how
you might try it still goes gorgeous—everything gagged
& stuffed scarlet with peeled pomelos, wrapped
in leaves of the evergreen. We were orange
with the ghosts of good things last night. You
should have seen the sweat of still-being-alive.
Everyone believed in healing through fire,
the polished-sheen of a rainbow trout held out
of a car window to dry in a summer wind.
Marshmallows torched too long, then lifted
blaze-topped to a blackberry sky. So lets elasticate!
Ask to take me home where I'll bite your earlobe
up & down before you make me stand all night
in the sparkling light of your kitchen dropping mugs
into the lukewarm sink water while you take
pictures of my bare backside. Butt. Spine. Butt.
Flash. Flash. Flash. But I know even before
your keys touch the lock you'll change
your mind & force me out of the hatchback
by the park where the moon moving
like a terrific skipping stone across
the river is orange, beautiful orange. I'll swear
I saw someone drowning, singing the same song
you hummed when your finger first touched
my thigh. So before it all happens, let me
tell you what you're getting us into. Let me look

you in the eye & tell you what I believe now
that I've fallen down the stairs dozens of times.
Count my fingers! Dozens of times!
Hurrah for how I wake crumpled & alone
with a torn-up pack of smokes stuffed
in my mouth. The gauzy light of marionettes
everywhere when I blink my eyes.
Even I'd laugh if I now said something
about the sweet hereafter, so open up, put this
on your tongue—& now that you have
one more tooth, think about vapors—
funnel clouds. High & tight fastballs.
How easy evolution is—the gorillas, standing
with their fists on their hips are watching *you* eat.
Sex symbols dangling from cracked rearview
mirrors. Like handcuffs. Like atomic numbers
holding their thumbs out in the rain. Arms
waving big X's in the thirtieth story window
of a high rise fire. A downpour that lets you see
through all the gristle to our real faces.
Howdy, please. Howdy. Now tell me you've lost
your legs so I know you'll really stay.

Good Times

Strangers will spring from parked cars
and howlingly sprint toward our children,
leveling the snowmen the kids are rounding out
with their mittened hands, leaving them
holding a carrot grown limp in the cold.
It's a fact: someone will unknowingly carve,
on the back of a bus seat, a secret equation
that might let us live forever, but the next
teenager who sits will scribble
a speaking penis over it with a felt-tip pen.
Like drive-by shootings, most of our good
ideas arrive, get a look at our crusty
mouths, then leave as fast as they came.
A creep is, at this very moment, staring
into the sliver of light that is your bathroom.

But *sigh*—this is the lesser of two,
as they say—the neonatal is still
at the hospital, warming under a heat lamp,
and the man the thug almost mugged
is now standing at another bus stop
miles away. For a limited time
all-of-us is playing at a theater near you.
The boy with glass bones becomes a karate
champion so he can save his mother
from her indentured servitude
in the fantasy service industry.
Droughts. French maids. Acid
rain. Locusts. And James Brown always

unburied and in the cartoons. Thousands
of first kisses will happen as the bulbs
dim and our globe warms with teeny-
bopper moans and steam. More
and more butter for all of us fatties,
and the cherry blossoms just past peaking
as we leave, blinking and rubbing our eyes
at the innumerable stars in the sky—staggered
as petals spinningly fall upon our misdiagnosed
shoulders. Our lips slick and salty. Our bellies
sloshing with all the soda we can drink.

Spotless

I love the suds—how the duck head peeks
Into the open-windowed sunlight through
The foamy bubble bath. But if you really must
Know, I wasn't there—in my head
I was slamming a car door and walking
Along a wood-chipped footpath to the river.
Old, shattered windows—some of the glass
Pink edged—rose from the trees and brush,
Reflecting, for a moment as I passed,
Half pictures of someone that pretty
Much looked like me except: no cuts
And bruises! From the sky fell
Hand-sized ceramic bats. So strange,
You said to me, to see the leaves
Still so green. I thought I might be
Able to love you forever. At the river
The same wannabe was pretending
To be Jesus, tossing his wet hair back,
Raising his arms in the air. Touchdown!
Touchdown! you yelled stripping away
Clothes as you ran and dove in—
Outside a car door slammed. The
Cat jumped to swat the door-
Knob. I called out the names of things
I hadn't seen in a long time—kimchee!
Syrup dripping from a smiling mouth!
A lipstick-kissed note that says *Don't*
Let Me Go Out Like That—Shriveled, I coursed

With jubilance until the crisp shells of the beetles
That floated in my pink lake bobbed against
My thighs, and my riven toes brushed and tugged
The bandages that were clogging up the drain.

Elevator Music

Lately my face does not feel like my own.
Lately my face feels like a tattering of rotten
leaves sewn. Lately my face does not feel.
Lately my face. Lately it doesn't get better
no matter how hard I try. Lately my face.
Lately the best things are free and I've forgotten
what it means to stand beneath an overpass
listening to passing semis as the fields of summer corn
shine, and off in the distance smoke from a fire
on the city's edge into the sky puffs. Lately my face
cannot tell, so it feels so much. Lately my face
is tied down and touched. Lately my face and I'm leaping
up each time someone points because I must
confess that springmelting sorrow I found when I brushed
my tongue at the very top of my throat right before driving
up the street to get the paper. Lately my face is not
the one and the girls at that gas station looked
like the miracles that came were not the ones they wanted.
Lately the lights go out in my face and in their steel-
framed glasses I saw colossal nights of chains
and whips. Lately, my lately face needs and I can
only see when the lights go out and then they handed me
pamphlet after pamphlet while I sipped charred coffee
and chewed a Danish. O lord, my face feels too close
to the moon and stars, I said in my head, my feet ache
but let's pretend it's my soul. I nodded my face
when their mouths stopped. My face does not feel
in the end, I said, but I love the trees and koala bears
and babies flying from passing cars—I went on and on

as she tried to smile slowly, stepping away. My face
not feeling above the mountain on the dashboard
and all of it was just gum, I realized as I drove away,
nothing but gum and darker moles of dirt. Darker. Darker.
Not feeling my face and darker. And like light,
my face in the heat molded so tightly around
the fist I sunk into it, driving so fast with only one hand
was so terribly difficult I knew I wouldn't be able
to make the sharp turn, and now, with my face,
just a rivulet of rain down the smashed up
visor of my helmet can shatter me again—
the beauty of this place bursting before
and behind and blueblack through my eyes.

Orgazo MoMo

after O'Hara

I wish that I might be different but I am
That I am and all that I have are my legs

Which, in truth, are arthritic heartbreaks
Feebly moonwalking through this sea

Of driftwood buntings Will you sink
With me, tasting my hand You must hold

Your breath Slow your pulse
To the gonging Please show me all

Your bling-bling Can you hear my
Chest's sump pump Its *I'm so strong enough*

Though it seems to be begging
Your pardon I am new

To this underwater adventure
Where sanctuary is sewn

From jellyfish and palm flesh
Jump in I'll speak intimately

To you the secrets of the lost city of wet
Throats—how down there, the light in our mouths

Is all flotsam and when you somersault
The seaweed shines like Vegas I promise

We'll be the return of cold showers Savior of midnight
Smoke breaks Time off for bad behavior

Dourine

Don't you think it'd be cool if we hung
        out? I mean, I once pulled

all of my fingernails off with my father's pliers,
        and still slivered the avocado perfectly—

you should have seen that salad. Grape
        tomatoes, red cabbage—I let the cold

water run over the cucumber in the colander
        until the tears on my face had dried.

The only thing I miss about those days
        is the morning light—how I could see

time countdown like a tiny digital clock
        on the necks of all the people I loved.

Everyone was trying to be the best
        animal they could be. Everyone wore

sundresses. Now, to be honest with you,
        I mostly stare blearily at mannequins

in the fancy stores downtown. One of these
        times I swear, with just the twitch

of an eye, a finger popped from inside
        my lip—I'll make one of those plastic

bastards come alive. I'll do anything you want
me to do, anything at all for my sixty seconds

of pain. Look: red boots! And matching lipstick!
I feel all of your love! And beneath this

ice-cream-cone-painted rain slicker—I just might
not have a lick of anything on.

Better Cleaning with Voodoo

Before cruelty pours like concrete
into the ravine between belly button & chin,
love's tiny tumbleweeds thud the ribs.
Lamely, they plink & plunk like stoned molecules
coming down. No room for regret,
they roll en masse like Hells Angels
on spine rides of passion crimes.
Not yet rotten cabbage, the heart glows
like a pearl beneath a pier, a jellyfish
squeezing away. This space is the body part
with no name. Paradise of heartbeats.
So booming teeth crumble, ears collapse.
Flick the belly button until it flattens
into a dimly lit stage. Watch the lung's pink
curtains swish away, uncover a woman
in top hat who saws herself in half.
Doves pull lipsticked questions
from her eyes as her breasts tumble. Voila!!—
albino tigers lick each other to music
that steams like cheek to cheek
in a hailstorm, & *POOF*—the sky falls
off its hinges. The lights grow bright.
It's the end, you think—you're winnowing
your clubfooted way to heaven
when the spotlight focuses like winter
sucker-punching spring. & there I am,
giving the world the finger as I blow

you a rebellion of kisses in hope you'll love
all my failures. Furiously, they scrub
the abracadabra off my body as I wink & smile,
smoking in this bathtub burning with leaves.

Sizzler

when things aren't right
I'm a happy hobo, red
fleshed with the terrible
& relentless clink of train spikes
beating sparks from each other
behind the calcified grain
of my breastbone—imagining
a breathtaking sunrise over
the inflatable pool my friends
break their necks diving into
while I watch, licking my
wounds like a dog in the shade.
buckets of milk swim
around my innards for
the benefit of my tapioca-
strong bones and the bees
churr around my mouth.
one nerf football teeter-
totters down the front steps
& a rough breathing glow
reflects off the aluminum
of the screen door. from where
I'm lying on the lawn
I can see it all: hanky panky
or cannibalism in the clouds,
flat-topped hedges and hibiscus,
a grandfather clock wheeled
out of the neighbor's place.
the off-beat chime as it rolls

announcing a new hollowness
to all of the street. the awful
smelling trees. flies riding
the failing light
of my breath. pollen
oranging my hands
like I'd been cutting
meat all day.

The Lights Go On The Lights Go Off

The perfect words are the ones that make
you cry—oh plate glass windows
waterfalling in sheets. Witnesses raise fists
wrapped around chicken bones. Thighs.
Drumsticks. Their lips sheeny with grease.
Then you tell the world everything
you've done wrong and thank god—
sirens and squeals and slamming doors.
Taser forks lodged in your neck. The light
comes down bulby and thick now—exploding
like Xmas tree ornaments thrown
into a bonfire and just as you go black
everything out there on the horizon
is fluttering. Before you wake you pass
through many nameless towns atop
a convertible, waving to the crowds
like it's a homecoming parade. Each main
street fades like night swallowing
the kids at the park until all you hear
behind you are basketballs being dribbled,
dribbled, then shot. You are lost
somewhere in it all as they stand
above you working their thumbs
through their key rings like janitors.
Thinned silk are the threads of your
shirt. The buckle on your jeans is coral.
Your skin is the color of something carried
at parties so fancy the balustrade is lined
with pearl. Someone above you is thinking

about how they need to pick up vacuum bags
before they go home to Randy. And as your hand
twitches their minds turn an inch, and like a fact
rising from another life, that same face above you
is bewildered into gibberish by the brawling drops
of the street lamp's sodium, the crests
of glass swathed out like a palm
frond over the sidewalk's red-caked cracks.

Something Wicked This Way Comes

The whimpering light in front of you is skipping.
That pulse in your head is a fat sledge. The exhaust

Smell, you think, hand cupping your mouth, really is
Your breath. And then you get it—this

Is what happens when all you can remember
Of language is a grunt: no ways to describe

The cracks in your windshield, a bowling ball nestled
Into it—How they look like the throat veins

On the three-fingered man you saw rake a broken bottle
Down his cheek as you sat paste faced at a bar in California.

You are nervous so you glance around, try to whistle
Through your teeth. You blink—noticing the still-throated birds

Locked dark in the trees. The sky is an unplugged
Blue. The sun's going west. Past the power lines,

Past the thorn-topped hills. Past where you've never
Been, or even, some chest-shattered day, wish to go.

Bedbugs

It'll be daybreak when we sing
So big eyed and throatless—gulping
In the wooly space of kissing one's elbows
Or blowing a kiss-my-ass at the sky. Mother's
Cheeks suffer from gravity and I
Am feeling lumpy in the armpit.
In the shower with no water
Running, I rotate my knuckles
Against what might be cancer
Or the remnants of my thoughts
On the fog rolling below the bridge. Words—
Carve them out of my throat and give me
My change. Throw the coins into the sun
And you've invented a new science
To save us from all this
Pushing and breathing. And then—
Just the sound of a stone skipping its white space
Above the water will pass you
Through night, remind you of the webby crust
You came from. But always a fly sits
On the counter and I have to wipe
My fingerprints from each glass. Just in case.
Who might understand this X
In my chest? That O? And in tonight's
Lilac-lit night—a light winking in the distance
Hope that someone might still be awake
The soft touch of an eye opening and closing
In invitation. A warning of an approaching storm.

Interview with a Ghost

This ink. This name. This blood. This blunder.

Terrance Hayes

the misery music is steaming on the front burner
    O how it blips & boils
its end-of-a-life-again song   the utensils are all
    scoured & the butternut's turned

O pounds of salt & sugar   hands splayed
    over breasts   meat in the icebox
& tomatoes stretched taut
    but it's rummaging in my head

how I replay it all   a motorcycle halved
    by a train: today it's dirt poured
into a bubble bath   dinner bells: the last pulse
    of an EKG   how I'd give

whatever paradise might be next
    for the tar-papered roof above me
to blaze   O the bringing of blood
    for if it's resentment to know

what are the living supposed to do
    hunching at this party next to a painting
of lovers eating fruit   bodies never separating
    or dying   while I can't get myself

under the whirr   before you go
   please: let me finish   they anointed
the surgeon's hands   but still
   the boy didn't ever return

to the surface   listen to it
   roaring outside in the trees—what's going on
in there   it hisses
   is everything   good?

l Love Cake

Unbuckle, unbutton, unzip. Set
the blender to frappé & spit.

Sing cellar mouth—in the kitchen
a wet hand fingering your thigh.

This carnival where we must lick—
slurp at the sunshined steak's thick drip.

Mix together in a sheet pan: a sugary
ache shaved from a snapped rib.
Bruises that are all twice baked.

Broil & julienne—the tongues
of lost secrets: flipper
arms, the myth of money & fish.

Now   sprinkle & wish   forever:
for it's the feast of failures. Gashes
down the chest like ties.

Open wide for the power
cords, fingertips humming with nails—

for there are wonders
the world should not see.

There's blood pooling
beneath the table—

alleluia, asshole, amen.
Together: let us eat.

Hallelujah Blackout

The self is no mystery, the mystery is
That there is something for us to stand on.

We want to be here.

The act of being, the act of being
More than oneself.

George Oppen

I

Zippergiven & stained I go
   Blankly broken
     & gazing for rain—

Wishing & wishing as the day lugs

Crenellated clouds across this city
   Crumbling loudhailed

With asphalt & shine—   A plover

Puzzles the salmonberries
   Where I wander

Waiting openhanded for old bodies
   To fall seamless
     From heaven to failed heaven

. . . . .

Be stunned   the dark hymns
   In this dollhouse

   I promise   *your giving*

It up will be fine   *for the scars*

     Are corded with forgetting

. . . . .

& all of this happens each midnight—   mayflies hardening
   The lampposts
   Bruised purple & weeping
   Under skinny-boned trees   with no words
I go mercy faced   & everything to me whispers   *no biggie*

   Motherfucker   we'll break you too
   Infested finally   & terrible   in the knuckle-branched black

   . . . . .

This wreckage is what's left to churn
Darkly away— O bewailing & pitted America—staring

Out & pointing from the penumbral flicker of picture windows

   . . . . .

   The blues thicketed along the riverbank

   Nostril wiping—Words slapped frail
Against my stewed & rainmaking heaven

A wet mouth lipping apple slices from a pocketknife
Because always there is a better low-pitched whistle
   Below the waves

   The rain tilting hard & never
   Below the waves

   No popping   No ruckus

A shock of blossoms abuzz
In sickness & in health

. . . . .

Where city lights like fireflies diving the water murmur
What happened to your shivaree   Shine

The lightninged hall   Of kisses
In the ballady veins—

O to be reborn a crush of ghettoed plowings
With a litter of still puppies   In the stapled head

Stone after stone wings
Into the slurping shadows

Silhouettes cuff the agony-boxed air

. . . . .

In that honeycombed
Pocket of night

Above the city's steeples
I fail irresistibly

To the lightswarm—
The whorl

Of stars wallpapering the sky
    & how I swerve

Spilling   over
    The leaf-strewn

& yellow-teethed streets
    My crooked & rotten-

Peached body—
    Hallelujah I gasp wearily

When I fall hard enough—like a barge
    Of revolving smoke

    Sashaying down
      A valley—
Not to know why

II

Outside my window   Brittle sticks turreting
    the shingled rooftop among a clutter

Of bucking birds   Boughs at the window scratching
    away another of night's darkenings

The radio as loud as it goes—an old bowl of milk tramping
    across the table—& this helps more

Than the pillsong   Hands across my face
    memoried with chocolatey blood

I have to remain   My face I slap
    over & over & over

. . . . .

    I hear nothing when I come back gasping
    & have to steady against the pane—

    & touching the window's early-morning
    Ironwork my fingers are bonerack & ink

Come out   mumbles the pipes rusting on & off   *Come out*

    & the soap & shaving cream
        Swirl & quake—X-rayed eclipses
            In front of me   Sweet Jesus

    I'm right here   I say to the paste-splotched mirror

Nightsweat dripping–
        My blackheart & cosmos

    . . . . .

Under that shower's mizzle the wood-
Wormed altarpiece in my hands
        Is my head

Dissevered with what
    I barely remember
        Tomato–Cane–Machete

            Names half-realized
            Through mouthfuls

            Of burning dirt   on nights
                Beneath the walking vines falling

            Their barbed & luminous emergencies

All fucking night

III

Backwards bending nothing rises
Out of me when I go to lose

     Myself on the river sinking
     Crunched cans & listening to rabbits

Swifting through the elmbrake   Stripped birches flung
   & floating away

   Grace notes wickeding the latticed-lit trees

As they miraculously fill   The chirps   The chirps
   Shotgun shells & a bible stitched of leaves—
      The first psalm of which
      Sings of the contour
      A body makes in rivermud

. . . . .

O song of a shape that sings: honesties
   Of a body sleeping
Twisted in front of headlights
   White sheeted—

Night beetles already eating
   Through the gluey-flesh
Bleating figures on the edge
   Of the charmed glow

All of it—black-&-white
   Photographs—
      Beautiful & still
        With hewing

  . . . . .

Which held to the swinging bulb   are hollow open
   & always   my ice-boxed insides
Swan-stitched   for whomever wants a tumble
   Plumbers & strangers

With halos & wings   I beg   forever
   Ecstasy   I beg
For more scars & moths fluttering a sill
   In the sunshine—   a sad lone voice

Uttering breathily through morning
   A cry   that starts beautifully
A violin sawing in the head   of anything
                That hears it

   I beg & beg   for good blessings
         & blackout the world

  . . . . .

So up from my back in the yard I have to be
   Picked away from the stars

That fine therapy—
The thrashing roll
　　Of an empty wheelchair cruising down the hushed street

　　　　This pockmarked　　Tongue

Clucking blood when it grinds on by

IV

Powdered & tasseled with blackash in the morning
A marching band trumpets & taps messily
Down the neighborhood football field—drumrolling
       On & on & on while I brim—

Because these almondy bones still hope & fear
      For the fucking bliss of it all

      I'll promise if I must—I promise
      To sink tender at midnight:

 . . . . .

Because the bottom is dropping out   In my waiting room
   So vibrant & easy coming   *You're sick again*

It says   *You'll get sicker*   *& believe me*
   You will get sick &   *Don't call when you do*

For I will not   *Take care of the bleedy leak & trickle*
   It is vibrant in the waiting room   It is coming

From the sickness   *Don't call me when you do*
   You will get the honey seep & dribble

Don't call me vibrant   *While you wait*

      You will get sick & sicker

V

The afternoon stoned black with rain
     & the shadows slash

Prayers are chanted behind soaked handkerchiefs:
     Let every thing be sugar cured

But it never will be forgiven
     The riverbank's lilacs are torn

When the rain drives into breakdown
     & there it is—

The jeweled lightning & I am

On the shore's river-pitted ruins
     Where no one can be

Beautiful   Suckholes & stones   So beautiful

   Below the citybright
     & everywhere exhaust

As steel-heavy sheets whiten the banks with rain

   Until above the bridge   The tremulous   Wrenching

Away of the failing day's clouds   & over the water flashes
        The symphony of firework
        & I am forever listening
        To the sky break ribs   As it bursts just
                Before my finger-socketed dark—
                Iron lunged & orange

VI

When I woke in the middle of the night dancing
Slowly   I thought the war must have been over
& I saw in front of me my breath hiving
In the air   But the throngs of children

With severed ears trying to sing on the midnight news
Sundered the bluish dark—Made me wonder
What dank heap with polished flies—What music
        They'd bawl when I was found

         The feathered smoke of underwear
           Varnishing a chair back
              Shadows blackpurple & scurrying

      & I couldn't stop weeping   In the shower

    I scrawled   With my tongue dance steps
            & the names of disasters
            On the misted glass

   . . . . .

The water's tongue-fever broadcasted the body luminous
   more calenture than ecstasy
Billow went the blood   wanton & blaze
   O mooncalfed stirring

O luminous fever turning the melody with blood
   shouting the lung thrills

& burn against sleep   a wink
    & match made beauty

& blood spilling through the sheets   O resplendent
    with chills   O ecstasy
Just a flash made beauty   billow & blaze
    turned blisters to calliope

  . . . . .

The hung dangle crack-necked
    & magnificent from the August moon

So I stir up something better & holler at the running
    Shapes that flash in & out of the street lamp

I can't imagine my molars humming more superbly—
    A chest any colder   Empty enough

    To bury everything inside me—

    I sleep with my feet above my head
        So the autopsy is naughty with light

VII

Gloss-necked with rain
   From wandering the boulevard
Where the wind-beat box elders yawp
    The whale-swallow
   & the sun does not crane—

Hail sluices through the ragged storm windows
& the house is a disaster of guttered ribbings

In the dark without power   I soak up the mess
Dipping again & again with old boxer shorts   But sway

Listening to the city's sirens   I squeeze the glass shards
Standing over the still thing that has flown through the window

Hunching   I bring it to my face & closer   How I care

    About the dead things I collect

. . . . .

       In that half sleep where I am   Overjoyed
       When lovers in the ravine plummet like lead

       Ingots   Heavensfallow hoistless
       & always danger   Atop that hummock

    Of deceit   I can almost remember: breath can be

    Simple   The pitchforked touch
       Let's shiver through that light   *light kiss*

VIII

Pooling on the back step of my throat in the morning—
The snap of stained sheets on the line watching crows

Clean something that used to live in the garage's rackety shadows
    Next to the garden   It's the spleening light of dreams

For the blooming green is dappled & charged—sewagesweet
     & I close my eyes again & sing

        O little demons   Baby
          O poor little lamb—

    Hoping the children are not stripped & hammered
To trees   & there are laughs & echoes

        O bound up   *Baby*
         & brilliant—
   The red shapes
Of their skinned necks & knees

IX

Over the bridge where each wave on the river is a call
For help   Chest thumping & the other sad glories

Stilled in the ragged robin   Down the river
The banks smell of rot   Thickening

With burnt cardboard & screwworm—sweat
    Running down sunburnt spines

Go ahead—ask   It's a broken nose
Bad luck   A spoon in the pocket

Flecked with something   No one can name
The days do not stop or stay   Such small

Leavings   The waves crunch   Again & again
The light is a rackle of shredding   Back

Go the eyes & I'm gone   The barges slouching
Heavy in this killing season   Two dogs

Stain the limestone with piss & the chicken wire rusts
    While the horned larks oil cake the bare trees

Everlasting rainouts   I give names to them all
    Evernumb & lowloving   All this life invulnerable

. . . . .

Who is the king of this place
The children sing   Tin cans

Crunching & I'm heron gutted
With the fineness of being filled

With smoke & still smoldering
All in & waiting: growing pale & less

Under the sure bet of the sky's broken light
The squall of car doors always slamming
            Over the sidewalk's cracks

To celebrate my Falling against it & believing   Out of breath
     The bruises beautiful in the city's music coming

     . . . . .

That ambulance song of bodies leaping   Skips & killick & skips
     & it's truckstop lung tonight among the candy swallowers

            Ribbons torn of flesh & horsehair harps
                Pinned & chiming against the screen door—

            Night is a cardigan of tombish voids & a jukeboxed moon

                The low-swinging magnolia will burn

X

Shivering at sundown I rock
       The reverie on the bridge's cresting
Light   Barking my shittalk
       To the pallet-giving wind

The pavement   with buses glistens
       Faces hammered & giving up
You'll all be undressed & under   The going-away
       Dark lisps sloppily & always

Another blink & everything inside me daggers
       City walkers outlined by fall's fading light
& the lamppost's waking bright shoots—
       Unsecret-ing the city park's slithering grass

While a spray of goatsuckers plunge
       Their winged flowering over the river
Twinned & rioting shimmers   Crocuses all hen tracked
       Cribbed leaves rumored with belief

   . . . . .

& leering at it all only makes
       The fist-shaking sky shred open
          In the most violent festival

     & I swear in the air   I taste jasmine
The body filling   With jolts until

     On the elms nothing can be carved again
Basketball-hooped scarecrows—Shadows slumping perfect

The happy-chopping music of night joggers
& the drinking fountains filled with horse flies

Yellow jackets burping up from the mud
& buzzard bait puddling the paths
Again & again it purrs through this falling den

Open your hands:

We have to cross one by one

. . . . .

The hard bells whirl over the creaked & broken hallways
Forever deadbolted & up circling

This ash-hearted & stammering America
Happy asshole alleluia
Chants the city's wrecked neon

Population:
Mashy kissing the mirror each morning—

Comforted by blankets sewn from sheet music
Orchestras of knives sopping red in the rain

Do you feel this
Being alive

. . . . .

For as long as I can I stare faun chested
      Into the eight-track sky

Like I've been punched
      In the Adam's apple

Wheezing I will be for you
      A honey bucket forever

Sleeping in this everywhere
      Slaughterhouse I go

Amongst blue dresses forever

   . . . . .

O hallelujah of cityglow waving   & ghosts' hands
      Gagging with sackcloth each night

        That ala kazam   Heavybright

      Finely split bones & bleeding faces
         Streaking the streets on fire

        For our disasters' brilliant purls
        For the down & sweet rolling

   . . . . .

      Let us sing that dark

      Real slow with the lucky

Understand that it can drink till it is
sick, but cannot drink till it is satisfied.

Frank Bidart

Patter to Mend

I measure time by how a body sways

Roethke

Through thorns, & a thick & wicked buzzing
   I sing nectar, a stumble
Born of itself & the moths all in flames
    & of course I'll show you my blood-nailed

Fingers   I sing blossom, brother,
    & all of my friends are pillow biters
Tails nailed to the walls & soup   Smell
   the burning hammers

They broken-worm like severed hands
   In a box of sea   For example: love
Me albinoed   For example: talk
   Down that sky unbettered

So, in this sparking light, what nervous tic
   Isn't possible? What gesture is it
Then, carved north to south down my chest?
   Don't be afraid   Take a look

Inside—   The contractions tractor & gleam
   Let us call it: real-live-bleeding

& sitting-in-a-chair-with-a-duct-taped-mouth

Why do we always want more & more & more?

All that angel dust speckling the fruit

In This Best of All Possible Worlds

I tried going a whole week without lying

I became both Boy Scout and Brownie

Campfire stories were told of my days as a cowboy

In X-rated movies. We ate so many cookies so soon

Sadness spread without a hunting permit

The sky opened into a secret evil

All mine, that hope-hat and fear-jelly

They couldn't understand my private language

How the nearer you get the more

The bagpipes become. And then the rain of teeth

And just to be loved we had to be little

Of what we wanted, and so damn dismally new

With our black lipstick and cherry bombs

The Meat Grinder

How we
     Got punched

& punched & punched
& I'd   love   to   again

But no one
     Said I am your father

I could have crushed him

        To bits
There was bread
       On the floor

& fruit on the floor & my arms

I could have made him piss
      His pants

I changed into a brand-new
      Shirt

& the ladies said *sweetie* & squeezed

There is a suitcase waiting
      In the hallway
Nobody will ever sleep

Plication

Birch-swinging boulevards & babies
Reflection kissing in strip-mall windows

& so today I will admit I try to forget
Damn near each minute of this life,

But can't shake the harmony trees cradle
In their veined heaven. Watch out

For the broken glass, kiddies!
& look at this! I carry my enormous head

In a backpack because I hate the fucking view!
From the sunset to way the hell over there

Pickups bucket over the concrete
So there might be hope somewhere

On the far side of this glory hole
But everything spins so fast

& in this town it's illegal to open
Your raincoat. The sky is a dentist drill

Flattening a magnolia & the clouds
Are chugging their tinny joy. My jaw

Is clenched & the traffic won't stop
Staring. Pray there are bandages

For this—that if I get down, peek
From my hands & knees

I'll hear the tense music—
That shine-forth, temblor, shine-through

Wildfires

when the last one went by
I waved and said so long—
all of the splinters shining
golden and charred in
my forehead. those shadows
really fly across the bus stops
when you run. when you
make it all for you. no matter
how I worked my chest
like a carjack, I couldn't catch
up to the others. so on the front
porch it was just-me time
with the bug-away candles
and the smoking car parts someone
had piled and not taken to the dump.
far away I thought I heard
a parade. a ball game. sirens.
the street looked pinched
to black on one end when I
chewed. I let the air sit
on my knee and listened
to dusk creep up on me.
if I didn't know better
I'd have said that the cloud
of wrens that had settled
in the dead elm, and were now
thumping the ground like shot puts,
were going crazy, just crazy from the heat.

Asthma Attack

If it seems like there is a tint of hurt
In my eyes it's because a badger
Is chewing on my lungs

Like they're blood sausages, and when I dive
Down the barnacled fjord of my throat
To slip a blade in him all the lights

Blink out and I have to resort
To rubbing the inside of my genitals
For fire. Hello, is this 911?

I'd like to report a missing
And useless person. There are only two
Ways to survive an earthquake

And both involve your shadow
And a Spanish rooster. Hey man,
Quit stomping on my new suede

Legs. Down here, the loveshack's
Walls are graffitied with horse eyes.
The floor is sticky with melted

G-strings. High five! Way down
Low! Don't tell me you've filled
Pitchers with albino and leprous mice.

It's a little too late to once again beg me
To suck out the poison. Remember—swab
With alcohol and apply pressure.

Put said appendage above heart.
What sort of problem are you having, anyway?

It's Hard to Tell Who Will Love You the Best

Why can I not slip into the next room
& hopeful-shrug, perusing your collection
of dragonfly wings & blaxploitation flicks?

In a rambler fantastically different from this
I grew up with very bad teeth & an appetite
for drawing on things I wasn't supposed to—

family photographs, the calves of women
standing in line at the supermarket. For years
I've been cloaked finely with dust & germs

from the unswept tiles of this earth—who
knew I'd end up sometimes being a good guy
with the back-slapping hugs & Jesus juice & whatnot.

Of course—there are days I still sit in the Nissan, doing
the crossword during the drive-by, but mainly I need
to be taught how best to forget. How to stop

the toilet from singing because it won't be such
a long road now that all the bombs are falling.
F-Bombs. Smart bombs. Stuffing mailboxes

with cherry bombs. Too soon we'll huddle under
the sheets with flashlights at our mouths, weeping
as we tell stories about our endless grinchitude.

It might be the last thing we ever do. All of us
the same & on & on & then it's over. You might think
this is an uncool way to look at the fan whirling around

the bedroom ceiling, but standing on a ladder this close
to it, my voice goes rough sledding & no matter how dizzy
I get, I can't close my dried out & bleeding eyes.

Resurrection

After the outbreak of whooping
Cough, a clear-skied rain nourished
Our strawberry-horned tabernacle.
Conch shufflers and carnies,
We were the last frontier of multiple partners,
Prime-time specials about dolphin preemies.
I told everyone it would be much yolkier,
Gathered and slapped the tribe vigorously. All was well
For a bit with the totem building, but soon
The eye polishers stopped rubbing to criticize
The carpenters for their gold-headed hammers.
Then, everything went wrong with our understanding
Of belief, and the bucket men stopped
Rounding up slugs. They whispered evolution,
Caressed their lips on sleeping cheeks,
But everyone knew it was scurvy.
We camped below the old lady's window
The night before disbanding. We peeked and peeked.
Many left urine samples in the nasturtiums.
High schoolers arrived in the morning to pick
Up the empty cans. Science is hard, they said,
Distracted by the rock 'n' roll
Of mallards V-ing across the unenthusiastic sky.
Some of them looked high. Some wore Band-Aids
Over their noses. Prove it, I said, drawing
A double helix in the flower dirt with a stick.
In truth, I didn't care, and only wanted
To grieve and hope for my harem of draftsmen.
The bowel-heavy trees said everything

Might not fall into place. Miles away,
The friends I had named for how they cup
Water and lift it to their faces had grown wings
And were making themselves available
To the most beautiful and jealous of birds.

Fuck All This Merrymaking

I only went because there were too many pieces
Missing from the whodunit and microwaving
The can o' corn was not a good idea. Not at all.
I wasn't clean after mowing and the mastodon

Carved from the hedge was laughable, but
They welcomed me to the party with a chainsaw
Sculpture of myself, smashed wineglasses, poolside.
Cannons were erected to shoot the lake-eyed sky.

The same taxi passed again and again and soon
I didn't feel like I belonged. My water-gun was buttery
And wouldn't shoot as long as the others. So I lied.
Then I lay down. I wanted sex because of the name-

Calling. I thought of the many times I'd been laid off.
Then, this too, turned off, which made me wonder—
Thank you, thank you, I shouted at the people pretending
To be my friends. They clapped when the odor cleared

The room and I noticed a woman cracking
Fortune cookies and discreetly slipping the fortunes
Up her skirt. I imagined her lucky numbers and long-winded
Privates. She turned, asked about my private beach.

I said, yes, I am in the Air Force. Soar those special
Blue ones, all the sideways tricks. She fell
Like Charlie Chaplin so I shouted repeatedly
To make sure she heard me. For a half-hour I answered

Questions about radar while she flopped on the carpet.
I used sign language and stuffed hummingbirds
But when I danced the Dandy Badger, she took her arm
The way widows do at funerals—tucked chin

And seethed with a mouth of oysters, what you feel
Will never be enough—the flamingo and I must go.

My Pet Chicken

After dinner I went rooftop
to watch the pre-moon curl over the city—

the roof where dusk's brilliance
lends itself to pickpockets and hit-and-runs.

I was consumed by the gentle-headed flowers
that grew from the shingles' dark

slivers that meant tar, no tar, tar. When I tilted
my head just so, I discovered ten new species

of bat. The evening sky was more school
shootings and plug pulling so I leapt

in hope that fatigue might bring a bit of sleep—
the dark that tugs itself from its own wool-fired

throat like a mythic beast redone poorly
in past-midnight movies. My night-light

broke long ago so I gently held your head
to the stars to see my favorite underwater adventure.

Drilling Tiny Holes in My Head

Each morning, I am swollen tongued—throat tight
With the hocus-pocus of chainsaws ripping

Through the birch. It wants to bury me deep—that breeze
Waiting like a knife fight in my driveway. All night I plan

How best to sell myself at the pawnshop—my basket
Of gold teeth. That fish-bellied smell. But I'm so afraid

Of paradise I only sit in my room, vibrating
At the speed of light—exploding and reknotting

The DNA of my breath. I have, at the top
Of today's to-do list, one ounce of woman giving

Birth beneath a summer sky restless & struggling
With seizures. My good days, when I do make it

Past the drive, are filled with circling the block
Until one of the old folks collapses so I can rush

To give them mouth to mouth. Here is a spine
Torqued into a balloon animal, I say. Here is a car wreck

In my hands. Come with me tonight, my chocolate-
Smelling love. Let's whip white-hot coat hangers around

Until someone loses an eye. Don't make me
Shake my head like I'm tired of everything

But you. Darkness is whirling so fast
And it's much too late to patch me up.

Everything

Listening to the fast-forward of robins
This morning all I've been able to think
Is octopi. You bet—if I had more arms
I would crump in the middle of my own circle
Of whooping butane fire. Wouldn't you?
Since I started this new diet of mainlining
Windex my dreams have been crashing
So beautifully—last night I gasped
When the naked man busted through
The screen door where I was shuffling
The sticky pages of my Whimper and Bang.
It really must be this thigh-shooting life,
Because he didn't stop, only spun the spatula
That sat on the tabletop as he sprinted by.
When I woke I was still under
Ground eating dirt and prayers. So—
When you come around later, the porch
Will be locked, but don't worry, I'll leave
The side door propped open with my extra
Head. Shake from side to side
Real fast so you don't notice the flies.
But I must tell you—today I feel
A bit jittery because I just realized I might
Never see the sun set again—just the setting sun.
I promise I'll give you the hard winter
I have origamied in the ass pocket of my jeans
If you let me sleep in this here black hole
Until tomorrow's sweet, sweet boogaloo of light.

The Way It Is

Up here a woman plays piano—
Eyes closed, flaring the fingers of her left

Hand. She cannot stop thinking
About shape, the way clouds

Walked across the morning
Sky. In the bathroom a boy

Drops orange after orange
Into the bathtub—practicing

His out-of-my-hands. A tongue
Of water stretches over the cold

Metal. The red peppers taste of snow-
Covered bike seats. Stories are told about hats

And everyone clutches their bellies,
Pretending to laugh. Afternoon

Dreams fill with the running water
Of lovers' voices—too smoky

For weeping. A door creaks and
Slams again and again. Waking,

A stranger climbs the fire escape to the roof
And from the edge feels the hollowness push

Back as he spray paints answers
To our secrets into the vanishing sky.

Etiology

After these blizzards
An air like moth-eaten sheets
Swells my lungs—keeps me
Pacing. Branches rap bluegrass
From the windows. And there is
Breath's utter failing. Midnight
Pulls and so each night I tap
The frigid glass—
Is this touch-frozen
Or the last thought
I'll have? I watch cars
Shake past—
Faces hard and green
In the radio light.
I know each driver is dreaming
About how their name might
Ring in another's mouth.
This is below zero
And the engine in my chest
Catching. I cannot get
My head around
This impossible light.
In this wreckage
Of ice I can do nothing
More than rake my fingertip
Across my collarbone
Each time the red tenderness
In the oil-slick sky pulses
On and off—on and off.

Up

I understand this might sound
    like the worst place

       to be   faucets
          on fire
             at home

So I imagine it as running

Long needles
    through my body

Each time I step into sunlight

      lights swinging naked
         in the basement—
           darling

           it's on fire

& we are fabricated from millions
      of our mother's hands

The piano & I are smashkneed
& smoldering torn open for you

       to sing   branches
knuckling the glass

in this shiver I'll believe
         bright in anything

Chévere

In calling this born of a mouth
   We promise a blossoming of tears

      A paradise of wreckages: therefore handcuffed & hidden
      We are deerlike: split open & down

Lightning flourishes our faces—diamond lipped & always ruined
    For example, the body falling inside this body
    For example, a pail filled with manicured hands

Here then is amplification. Here they come
   With something in their mouths
& thought is limited by the crust
   That hardens around the lip of bottles

The harmony-throated are joy
   The rest are knife
One minute for tender & glory   No more

By night we know it for what is stirring in the dumpster
& now it is the long hemlock away
     The intimate x that doesn't y

  I then understand me buried in garden

    To this we say needle above & eye to eye
In contrast to buried-in-this-hole-for-a-very-long-time

This, it is told, came with a whole lot of high fives
And the more & the faster, the more real, the hotter
Which means that here, anything is possible

By touching, a thing becomes our someday-electricity-head
By *eternity* we understand the man pointing
      the woman collecting water
That pours from a slit-open cactus
      with an overturned crab-shell

& in this anything-is-possible world we only exist
    When whirling to go
We draw it all with our dirty tongues
    The stumps of our missing hands

Sawing Tinfoil

The spilled pitcher of dimes blazes the hollow & alone
        & denying face or body, the legless
                Dog recedes in the hammock

A hymn that has been stolen again & again by looking up, fisting
            The armless blue

            This striptease of leaves & flies

We have no answer for that which makes it clear that the throat
    Doesn't understand up or down

        Goddamnit, I am praying
          To be good

King of the honest-night with pitchfork
            & the sky splitting mirrored

Asleep in the yard. Asleep without silver lining
         & what you are not

Wishbone moon tugged loose from the living
            & voice stacked, haunting

    I won't go in the cellar if each part is twice
        As large again as belief
        As anything measured with a mouth

           Count & rattle them spoons

Switchblade the glass & heads spin. Inch by inch
The push is torn & bronzed into ripeness

For my tumbles, my pocketful of sharked-tremors

This rodeo skin & under weeping
One by one, dissolving

This is the factory of exactly right & wingless birds
A ghost that comes in the night
To caress endless snakeskins of trash

We will be divided into good times that must hang
Frozen hooked & high on amphetamines

Wet bits & dry bits, soft bits & hard bits
But none of these bits is punk rock

We have two ways of thinking about crying
We depict it as rainbowed oil or angels
Waiting in parked cars

It is all so easy now that everywhere light is the same
In this miserable heaven
Anyone who wants to come over can

Skin On Skin Off Skin On Skin Off

Because the rain did not stop humming
Our last words no one went out to disarticulate
The spine whipping from the clothesline.

It was a snake-eyed night and we were doomed
To swallow our hammered hands.
Just as that mole sits—a burned pearl

In the pinch of your eye or zigs are carved
In the crying girl's wrist—we must now chug
As much moonshine as we can, slapping

Our cheeks to pass out or blush. How it gives us
The sustenance and amnesia of bees.

Flash lighting. Bleached teeth. Savage animals
Mouthing oh-oh in sleep, we crumble on the floor,

Dreaming our blackjack as parades
Of manhole covers wobble
Down the alleys of our chests.

For weeks we'll sit in a bathtub
In the front yard, makeup clowny,
Banging our pots and pans

Like thoroughbreds. Damn it—
Our undertaking should be so much greater
Than a hummingbird bagged and cracked

With a boot. We've got everything you want
In the matchbook of our heads.

Oh, gutterglow—mutter it, mutter it again.
Make us savor the last word you speak.

Author photo: Ariane Balizet

Alex Lemon's first collection, *Mosquito,* which documents his slow recovery from brain surgery as a young man, was hailed by *Publishers Weekly* as an "edgy, energetic, even frenetic debut from a rising star of the Midwest." Lemon's poems have appeared in *AGNI, Black Warrior Review, Bomb, Denver Quarterly, Gulf Coast, Pleiades,* and *Tin House.* Among his awards are a 2005 Literature Fellowship in Poetry from the National Endowment for the Arts and a 2006 Minnesota Arts Board Grant. He is the co-editor of *LUNA: A Journal of Poetry and Translation* and is a frequent contributor to *The Bloomsbury Review.* He lives in Minneapolis, Minnesota.

More Poetry from Milkweed Editions
To order books or for more information,
contact Milkweed at (800) 520-6455
or visit our Web site (www.milkweed.org).

Music for Landing Planes By
Éireann Lorsung

The Art of Writing:
Lu Chi's Wen Fu
Translated from the Chinese by Sam Hamill

Astonishing World:
The Selected Poems of Ángel González 1956–1986
Translated from the Spanish by Steven Ford Brown
and Gutierrez Revuelta

The Phoenix Gone, The Terrace Empty
Marilyn Chin

Playing the Black Piano
Bill Holm

Willow Room, Green Door
New and Selected Poems
Deborah Keenan

Interior design by Wendy Holdman
Typeset in Rotis Serif
by Prism Publishing Center
Printed on acid-free recycled
(100 percent postconsumer waste)
Rolland Enviro paper
by Friesens Corporation